SCARF OR STOLE AT ORDINATION?
A PLEA FOR THE EVANGELICAL CONSCIENCE

NEW EDITION

ANDREW ATHERSTONE

The Latimer Trust

The Latimer Trust (formerly Latimer House, Oxford) is a conservative evangelical research organisation within the Church of England, whose main aim is to promote the history and theology of Anglicanism as understood by those in the Reformed tradition. Interested readers are welcome to consult its website for further details of its many activities.

The Latimer Trust
London N14 4PS UK
Registered Charity: 1084337
Company Number: 4104465
www.latimertrust.org
administrator@latimertrust.org

Contents

1. A Question of Conscience

'I can only say that from my knowledge of the Bench of Bishops, which is considerable, I think it is inconceivable that any of the Bishops would press an ordination candidate, contrary to his conscience, to wear a stole at his ordination.'

Archbishop Michael Ramsey, House of Lords, July 1964

Each year the same scenario is repeated in dioceses throughout the Church of England. Evangelical ordinands approaching the end of their initial theological training look forward with eager enthusiasm to ordination and curacy. A title parish is agreed and they are warmly welcomed by the bishop as part of the diocesan family, ready to be launched into a new sphere of public ministry. But then comes the letter explaining the practical arrangements for ordination in the cathedral. The dress code is clearly laid down – black shoes, black socks, cassock, surplice, and white stole. Immediately the ordinand faces their first dilemma in their relationship with their bishop. Shall they conform and wear the stole, or ask for permission to be excused this particular item of clothing, as a matter of conscience?

Clerical dress is, of course, an entirely trivial subject when compared to the many major issues of concern in the world and the church. The finer details of millinery on display in the cathedral is probably the last thing that should trouble the minds of bishops and ordinands when the proper focus is upon a public celebration of the Christian gospel and prayers for Holy Spirit empowered fruitfulness and faithfulness in a lifetime of ordained ministry. Nevertheless, there must be a dress code, and there always has been. The ordinal attached to the *Book of Common Prayer* states that ordinands are to be 'decently habited' when presented to the bishop. The *Common Worship* ordinal directs that, if mutually agreed, they may be clothed 'in their customary vesture' during the service, though whether the agreement is between bishop and ordinand or bishop and archdeacon is nowhere explained.[1] There are no further official guidelines and nothing laid down in canon law, so local diocesan custom usually prevails.

For most of the long history of the Church of England since the *Book of Common Prayer* was inaugurated, the typical dress code for ordinands has been a simple surplice, or a surplice and black scarf. Yet since the early twentieth century, in many dioceses, a surplice and white stole has become the norm. Every year this presents a crisis of conscience for some evangelical ordinands who object to wearing a stole on historical and theological grounds. Some bishops wisely and graciously welcome variety of custom, permitting ordinands to choose either scarf or stole. Others, unfortunately, do not. Their usual

---

[1] *Common Worship: Ordination Services*, Study Edition (London: Church House Publishing, 2007), 29, 51.

rationale is that the unity of the diaconate or presbyterate necessitates the visual unity of a common vesture.[2]

In Archbishop Ramsey's day he was able to assure the House of Lords that it was 'inconceivable that any of the Bishops would press an ordination candidate, contrary to his conscience, to wear a stole at his ordination.'[3] The same cannot be said of the Church of England today. In some dioceses evangelical ordinands find themselves strongly pressurised into wearing a stole and told that no exceptions will be made. If they resist the directions of the bishop, or the bishop's chaplains, it is interpreted as disloyalty or petty-mindedness. To the ordinands, at the outset of their ministry, the intransigence of the diocese can seem like cajoling or even bullying. Altogether, what should be a time of tremendous celebration for all concerned becomes a miserable experience, leaving ordinands feeling beleaguered and disaffected. This unnecessary and distressing conflict can easily be avoided by gracious allowance made for the evangelical conscience.

The purpose of this short booklet is to help bishops, evangelical ordinands and training incumbents better to understand the historical debates within the Church of England about stoles at ordination. After a brief

---

[2] See, for example, the Liturgical Commission's paper, 'Celebrating Ordinations: A Practical Guide', *Common Worship: Ordination Services*, 164–5.

[3] *Parliamentary Debates (Hansard): House of Lords*, 13 July 1964, vol. 260, column 51.

3

survey of the place of stoles within Anglicanism, at the Elizabethan Settlement and the Tractarian Revival, it focuses especially upon the history of stoles at ordination in the mid-twentieth century. Based on new research in the official papers of Archbishop Fisher and Archbishop Ramsey in Lambeth Palace Library, it examines the episcopal consensus and assurances of the 1950s and 1960s, which deserve serious re-consideration. It appeals for a return to the days of generous Anglican attitudes, whereby every ordinand is given freedom of choice over whether to wear a scarf or a stole.

2. Reformation and Ritual

To the casual and uninformed observer, a stole and a scarf look remarkably similar – both are a long piece of fabric draped over the minister's shoulders. Indeed the scarf is sometimes, incorrectly, called a 'black stole'. Yet viewed from the perspective of Anglican history, these two pieces of clothing are quite distinct, both in terms of their origins and their theological associations.

The stole was originally part of the complex array of medieval clerical dress, evolved from Roman antiquity.[1] It is a narrow strip of coloured silk, often embroidered and fringed at the ends, hanging down to the knees. Sometimes it is ornately decorated and embellished with three crosses, at the centre and both ends, and the cross in the centre is kissed by the minister before the stole is put on. The instructions of the Anglo-Catholic Warham Guild are typical: stoles are to be worn at the ministration of the sacraments in different liturgical colours – at baptisms and confirmations (red or white), at weddings (gold or white), when hearing confessions or anointing the sick (blue or violet) and when presiding or assisting at Holy Communion (in the liturgical colour of the day or the season). But for non-sacramental services, such as Morning and Evening Prayer, the black scarf is worn

---

[1] For a broad survey of changing fashions in clerical vesture, see Janet Mayo, *A History of Ecclesiastical Dress* (London: Batsford, 1984).

instead. So a scarf is worn at a funeral, but a stole at a requiem mass.[2] The black scarf, by contrast, originally known as the 'tippet', was part of medieval academic dress, worn with the academic hood and made of the same material.[3] It is a wider piece of fabric than the stole, and typically hangs down to the ankles.

During the English Reformation, stoles were explicitly abolished from the Church of England, along with many other medieval vestments, but surplices, scarves and academic hoods were maintained. For example, the injunctions issued by Archbishop Edmund Grindal of York in 1571 included stoles among a long list of church ornaments no longer permitted. He instructed:

> That the churchwardens and minister
> shall see that antiphoners, mass books,

---

[2] Leonard Spiller, *Stoles and Scarves* (London: Warham Guild, 1957), 6–7. For other classic Anglo-Catholic commentaries, see Percy Dearmer, *The Ornaments of the Ministers*, new edition (London: Mowbray, 1920), 62–4; Cyril E. Pocknee, *Liturgical Vesture: Its Origins and Development* (London: Mowbray, 1960), 21–4. For Roman Catholic perspectives, see A. Welby Pugin, *Glossary of Ecclesiastical Ornament and Costume* (London: Henry Bohn, 1844), 194–5; E.A. Roulin, *Vestments and Vesture: A Manual of Liturgical Art* (London: Sands, 1931), 132–7; Robert Lesage, *Vestments and Church Furniture* (London: Burns & Oates, 1960), 113–8.

[3] For discussion of the 'tippet', see James Craigie Robertson, *How Shall We Conform to the Liturgy of the Church of England?*, 3rd ed. (London: John Murray, 1869), 104–8.

grailes, portesses, processionals, manuals, legendaries, and all other books of late belonging to their church or chapel, which served for the superstitious Latin service, be utterly defaced, rent, and abolished. And that all vestments, albs, tunicles, stoles, fanons, pyxes, paxes, hand-bells, sacring-bells, censers, christmatories, crosses, candlesticks, holy-water stocks, or fat images, and all other relics and monuments of superstition and idolatry, be utterly defaced, broken and destroyed ...[4]

Of course, to some puritans in the Church of England, it seemed illogical to keep the scarf while abolishing the stole. They wanted to go further and erase both these traditional vestments. During the controversy surrounding the *Admonition to Parliament* in 1572, the puritan Robert Johnson complained to Bishop Edwin Sandys of London, 'You must yield some reasons, why the shaven crown is despised and the square cap received; why the tippet [scarf] is commended and the stole forbidden; why the vestment is put away and the cope retained; why the alb is laid aside and the surplice

[4] 'Archbishop Grindal's Injunctions for the Laity in the Province of York, 1571', in *Religion and Society in Early Modern England: A Sourcebook*, ed. David Cressy and Lori Anne Ferrell, 2nd ed. (New York: Routledge, 2005), 106.

is used'.[5] Likewise Thomas Cartwright, leading puritan nonconformist, asserted in his arguments with Bishop Whitgift that surplice and tippet were 'attire unmeet for a minister of the gospel to wear'.[6] Nevertheless, despite these puritan protests, black scarves were retained within the reformed Church of England because of their association with academic dress and thus with theological learning, a visual reminder of the need for an educated clergy equipped to teach the Scriptures. For this reason, the black scarf is sometimes known colloquially as the 'preaching scarf'. But stoles were abolished outright because of their historic association with medieval sacramentalism. Within the Elizabethan church, stole and scarf thus came to symbolise contrasting theological emphases. The scarf was immediately recognisable as the clothing of the reformed pastor, and the stole as that of the Roman Catholic priest.

The nineteenth-century Tractarian Revival brought stoles back into fashion in the Church of England after an absence of three hundred years. For an explanation of their significance, some Anglican liturgiologists like

[5] Robert Johnson to Edwin Sandys, 2 February 1573, in *A Parte of a Register, Contayninge Sundrie Memorable Matters, Written by Divers Godly and Learned in Our Time, Which Stand For, and Desire the Reformation of Our Church, in Discipline and Ceremonies, Accordinge to the Pure Word of God and the Lawe of Our Lande* (Middelburg, 1593; facsimile edition, New York: Da Capo, 1973), 104.

[6] Quoted in *The Works of John Whitgift*, ed. John Ayre, 3 vols (Cambridge: CUP for the Parker Society, 1851–53), 2: 1.

Within the Elizabethan church, stole and scarf thus came to symbolise contrasting theological emphases.

John Mason Neale looked back to the classic allegorical interpretations of Guillaume Durand, Bishop of Mende, in his *Rationale Divinorum Officiorum* (*c.*1292–96). According to Durand, the stole

> represents the gentle yoke of the Lord, which is the yoke of the precepts of the Lord, which he puts on his neck, so that he can show that he has taken upon himself the Lord's yoke. When he puts it on and removes it, he kisses the stole to denote the assent and desire to which he subjects himself with this yoke ...[7]

This symbolism was picked up by Charles Walker in his popular catechism, *The Ritual Reason Why* (1866), which explained that the stole 'represents the yoke of Christ'. Walker numbered the stole amongst the 'eucharistic vestments', along with the amice, alb, girdle, maniple, tunic, dalmatic and chasuble. He called the alb 'the sacrificial vestment', to be worn by the priest and his assistants during the offering of the eucharistic sacrifice.[8] The more advanced ritualist clergy were soon wearing stoles on many occasions, sometimes as a visual demonstration of their continuity with the

---

[7] *William Durand on the Clergy and their Vestments: A New Translation of Books 2 and 3 of the Rationale Divinorum Officiorum*, trans. Timothy Thibodeau (Scranton, PA: University of Scranton Press, 2010), 155.

[8] Charles Walker, *The Ritual Reason Why* (London: Hayes, 1866), 16, 18, 21.

catholic priesthood, sometimes as a party badge and an act of provocation. When Bishop Tait of London went to consecrate St Michael's Church, Shoreditch in August 1865 there was a large gathering of clergy in the vestry before the service, many of whom were wearing coloured stoles. Tait remonstrated with them, 'I must ask the clergy of my diocese who are here today, to wear the simple dress of clergymen of the Church of England', upon which they took off their stoles and replaced them with black scarves.[9]

During the Anglican 'worship wars' of the 1870s, stoles were formally declared illegal in the judgment against John Purchas, perpetual curate of St James' Chapel, Brighton. Purchas was a flamboyant ritualist and author of *Directorium Anglicanum* (1858), a detailed manual of ritual which again included the stole among the eucharistic vestments. The ecclesiastical Court of Arches was asked to decide upon the legality of forty-four different practices which Purchas had introduced, mostly concerning his conduct of the eucharist. In large part, the judgment of Sir Robert Phillimore (Dean of Arches), delivered in February 1870, rested upon an historical interpretation of the notoriously vague 'Ornaments Rubric' in the *Book of Common Prayer*, which reads as follows:

> And here is to be noted, that such
> Ornaments of the Church, and of the

[9] Randall T. Davidson and William Benham, *Life of Archibald Campbell Tait, Archbishop of Canterbury*, 2 vols (London: Macmillan, 1891), 1: 439.

> Ministers thereof, at all Times of their
> Ministration, shall be retained, and be in
> use, as were in this Church of England,
> by the Authority of Parliament, in the
> Second Year of the Reign of King Edward
> the Sixth.

This rubric was, in effect, an extract from the 1559 Act of Uniformity, one of the key legislative planks of the Elizabethan Settlement.[10] Much ink has been spilt on the problematic question of how to interpret this Elizabethan injunction, and what exactly was worn by clergymen in the second year of King Edward VI. After surveying the historical data Phillimore ruled, as part of a longer judgment, that stoles were illegal: 'It is unlawful, therefore, for Mr Purchas to wear or authorise to be worn ... stoles of any kind whatsoever, whether black, white, or coloured, and worn in any manner ...'[11] In reviewing the Purchas judgment, the Judicial Committee of the Privy Council went further in 1871 and declared the wearing of albs and chasubles also to be illegal, a verdict upheld in

---

[10] 'The Act of Uniformity, 1559', in *Documents of the English Reformation*, ed. Gerald Bray (Cambridge: James Clarke, 1994), 334.

[11] James Murray Dale, *Legal Ritual: The Judgments Delivered by the Privy Council and Dean of Arches in the Recent Cases of Martin v. Mackonochie and Elphinstone v. Purchas and Hebbert v. Purchas, with Notes and Suggestions for the Guidance of Incumbents, Churchwardens and Parishioners* (London: Effingham Wilson, 1871), 158.

1877 in the case against Charles Ridsdale, ritualist vicar of St Peter's, Folkestone.[12]

This obscure liturgical history need not delay us further. The point is simply that stoles were almost unknown within the Church of England from the Elizabethan Settlement until the Tractarian Revival. At the time of their re-introduction, they were closely identified with the Anglican ritualists. In fact, they were declared illegal in 1870 and remained so, technically at least, until the Clerical Vestments Measure in 1964. The tremendous success of the Anglo-Catholic movement, and its fashions in clothing, meant that stoles had become almost ubiquitous by the mid-twentieth century. They were readily adopted by many clergy outside the Anglo-Catholic tradition, who did not necessarily attach any particular significance to the garment.

Nevertheless, there has always been a significant number of evangelical parishes where stoles are not worn, for theological and historical reasons. For some evangelicals today, especially those well-schooled in Anglican history, the stole still carries connotations of Roman Catholic or

[12] For this background, see especially Peter Anson, *Fashions in Church Furnishings, 1840–1940,* 2nd ed. (London: Studio Vista, 1965); James Bentley, *Ritualism and Politics in Victorian Britain: The Attempt to Legislate for Belief* (Oxford: OUP, 1978); Bernard Palmer, *Reverend Rebels: Five Victorian Clerics and their Fight Against Authority* (London: Darton, Longman & Todd, 1993); Nigel Yates, *Anglican Ritualism in Victorian Britain, 1830–1910* (Oxford: OUP, 1999).

Anglo-Catholic theologies of ministry and priesthood. The fact that stoles have now been adopted across almost all theological streams within the Anglican family, and have been declared by canon to be without theological meaning, is not sufficient reason for historic evangelical concerns to be laid aside. Therefore, every year, there are evangelical candidates at ordinations in English cathedrals and parish churches across the country who are not willing to wear a stole. Their refusal to conform is not motivated by partisanship, but by a careful weighing of the historic connotations of the stole within the Anglican narrative. For these evangelical ordinands their rejection of the stole is not a question of personal taste or preference, nor of rebellion against authority, but of conscience, both historically and theologically informed.

3. A Forgotten Consensus

'As regards the wearing of a White Stole, for the future in no Diocese of the Church of England will an ordinand, who has been offered a title, be denied Ordination on the sole ground that he finds himself conscientiously unable to wear a white stole.'

Bishops' Statement, January 1953

The clash between evangelical ordinands and their bishops over stoles at ordination is nothing new. It has been an unresolved problem for over a century. Episcopal policy has varied from gentle persuasion to fierce rebuke, and even (most notoriously) outright refusal to proceed with the ordination. But a sensible and fair resolution is not hard to reach, and the bishops' guidelines in the 1950s, now largely forgotten, point the way forward. First let us briefly survey this history.

A. T. Houghton was a prominent leader within Anglican evangelicalism as general secretary of the Bible Churchmen's Missionary Society (now renamed Crosslinks) in the decades after the Second World War. As a young man he served as a pioneer missionary in Burma, after a curacy at Holy Trinity, Tunbridge Wells. Yet before his ordination as deacon in Rochester Cathedral in December 1921, Houghton was placed in an awkward position by Bishop J. R. Harmer who insisted he wear a stole. The ordinand refused as a matter of conscience, so the bishop challenged him over his oath of canonical obedience, but Houghton replied that this did not extend to the wearing of stoles. Harmer could not appreciate the evangelical position and ended the interview with a rebuke, 'I think you are very petty'. It was a distressing experience, on which Houghton reflected: 'I had felt like a martyr of the Inquisition at an auto-da-fé and my ordination which should have been such a blessing, was an utter misery.'[1]

Other ordinands had similar stories to tell of facing intense episcopal pressure. Bishop A. F. Winnington-Ingram of London played a game of 'chicken' with his ordinands, at Advent 1934, to test their resolve right up to the last moment. When three evangelical candidates asked to be excused from wearing a white stole, he made it clear that they would not be ordained and drew attention to their recalcitrance at the pre-ordination retreat at Fulham Palace. Shortly before they were due to depart for St Paul's Cathedral the three ordinands were sent for separately and asked whether they would now 'fall into line'. When they still declined, Bishop Winnington-Ingram allowed them to proceed to the cathedral after all, with the other candidates.[2] Bishop Richard Parsons

[1] Timothy Yates, *Pioneer Missionary, Evangelical Statesman: A Life of A.T. (Tim) Houghton* (Milton Keynes: AuthorHouse, 2011), 28.

[2] The three conscientious objectors were Cyril A.B. Carter (BCMS College, Bristol), T. Gregory Smith (London College of Divinity) and T.H.E. Woods. See letter from Cyril Carter, *English Churchman*, 2 November 1951, 549.

'I had felt like a martyr
of the Inquisition
at an auto-da-fé and
my ordination which
should have been such
a blessing, was an
utter misery.'

of Southwark likewise put 'relentless' pressure on Philip E. Hughes (later a prominent evangelical theologian) at his ordination in 1941. Hughes was chosen to read the Gospel because he scored the highest marks in the deacons' examination, but the bishop insisted it was 'an unbroken custom' at Southwark ordinations for the Gospeller to wear a stole. Only when Hughes refused, as a matter of conscience, did the bishop relent, the day before the ordination.[3]

Matters came to a head in the early 1950s. The new bishop of London, William Wand, was unwilling to make any allowance for evangelical consciences. At Michaelmas 1951, three evangelical ordinands were forced to submit to wearing a stole as a *sine qua non* of ordination, despite their pleas to be excused on grounds of conscience. The principals of the evangelical theological colleges appealed to Archbishop Fisher of Canterbury on behalf of their students, suggesting that their attitude to stoles, based as it was upon Anglican history, 'ought not to be dismissed as unreasonable'.[4] As one of the principals

[3] Philip E. Hughes to D. Gordon Mills (registrar of the Church of England in South Africa), 16 June 1941, 'Archbishop's Office, Correspondence Overseas, CESA', 1992/26/73, Sydney Diocesan Archives. I am grateful to Mark Earngey for this reference.

[4] Cyril Bowles (Ridley Hall, Cambridge), Donald Coggan (London College of Divinity), L.E.L. Roberts (Clifton College, Bristol), W.M.F. Scott (St Aidan's, Birkenhead), Julian Thornton-Duesbery (Wycliffe Hall, Oxford), L.F.E. Wilkinson (Oak Hill College), J. Stafford Wright (Tyndale Hall, Bristol) to

put it, although he personally was not troubled by stoles, he thought it 'unjust that a man should be refused ordination simply on the grounds of conscientious scruples about wearing something not required by the Church of England'.[5] Likewise H. A. H. Lea (president of the Bible Churchmen's Missionary Society) advised Fisher that it was wrong to force an ordinand to act against his conscience 'upon the most solemn occasion of his life'.[6]

The following year the crisis deepened. In Salisbury diocese, an evangelical ordinand due to be curate of St John's, Weymouth, was refused ordination by Bishop William Anderson because as a matter of conscience he would not wear a white stole.[7] In Oxford diocese, Michael Farrer (former president of the Oxford Inter-Collegiate Christian Union and graduate of Tyndale Hall, Bristol) was due to be ordained at Advent 1952 as curate of St Ebbe's, Oxford. Bishop Kenneth Kirk refused to ordain him without a white stole, but did grant Letters Dimissory

Geoffrey Fisher, 5 January 1952, Lambeth Palace Library [LPL], Fisher Papers vol. 132, fo. 70. For the bishops' discussion of this letter, see Minutes of Bishops' Meetings, 14–15 January 1952, LPL, BM 13, fos 104–6.

[5] W.M.F. Scott to Fisher, 26 January 1953, LPL, Fisher Papers vol. 132, fo. 87.

[6] H.A.H. Lea to Fisher, 16 November 1951, LPL, Fisher Papers vol. 92, fo. 171. See also letter by H.A.H. Lea, *English Churchman*, 12 October 1951, 512, and subsequent correspondence until 4 January 1952.

[7] 'Bishop Rejects Student', *News Chronicle*, 5 March 1952, 1.

so that Farrer was ordained instead by Bishop Christopher Chavasse of Rochester for ministry in Oxford.[8] In London diocese the situation was more deeply entrenched. Before the ordination at Michaelmas 1952, six evangelical candidates expressed their difficulties about wearing a stole. After persuasion by Bishop Wand, four agreed to conform, but two still refused as a matter of conscience.[9] Both were graduates of Oak Hill College, Derek Elliott and Norman Dunning. Elliott had already served for a year as deacon at St John's, Ealing, having submitted to wearing a stole at his ordination the previous year. But his conscience was troubled, and he resolved not to do the same again.[10] Dunning had accepted a title post at St Andrew's, Whitehall Park, and had moved into the curate's house with his wife and two young children in preparation for ordination.[11] But when these two men

---

[8] Stafford Wright to Fisher, 7 November 1952; Michael Farrer to Fisher, 11 and 20 November 1952; Fisher to Farrer, 18 November 1952; Fisher to Wright, 18 November 1952, LPL, Fisher Papers vol. 109, fos 66, 68, 75, 79, 86.

[9] William Wand to Fisher, 19 November 1952, LPL, Fisher Papers vol. 109, fos 83–4.

[10] Donald R. Hill to Fisher, 18 September 1952, LPL, Fisher Papers vol. 109, fos 50–1.

[11] Norman L. Dunning to Fisher, 22 October 1952, LPL, Fisher Papers vol. 109, fo. 59. For his training incumbent's appeal to the Archbishop, see H. Mark Russell to Fisher, 12 November 1952, Fisher Papers vol. 109, fo. 72. For his father's appeal, see Alfred E. Dunning to Fisher, 28 January 1953, Fisher Papers vol. 132, fos 92–3.

declined to wear a stole, Bishop Wand refused to ordain them and told them to find curacies in another diocese.

The Archbishop of Canterbury privately urged Wand to solve this pastoral crisis by offering Letters Dimissory as Kirk had done, but Wand was intransigent and both ordinands were forced to leave.[12] Elliott was 'deeply distressed' at this enforced departure from his parish.[13] He was taken under the wing of the Bishop of Coventry, who ordained him priest in 1953 to a second curacy near Leamington Spa. Dunning had to wait until Trinity 1954 to be ordained deacon by the Bishop of Southwell to a curacy at Lenton in Nottingham. To the friends of these two evangelical ordinands, the Bishop of London appeared guilty of 'an awful exhibition of unchristian behaviour'.[14] No doubt there was fault on both sides, but the relationship between bishop and ordinands had broken down irrevocably, causing pain to all concerned. Meanwhile in his chapel at Fulham Palace, Bishop Wand commissioned new murals in 1953 from Brian Thomas, including a prominent depiction of the stoning of St Stephen (Acts 7) showing the martyr vested in a white alb and a red stole, fixed deacon-wise from his left

[12] Fisher to Wand, 24 October 1952; Wand to Fisher, 27 October 1952, LPL, Fisher Papers vol. 109, fos 61–2; Fisher to Wand, 15 January 1953; Wand to Fisher, 19 January 1953, Fisher Papers vol. 132, fos 79, 81.
[13] Derek J. Elliott to Fisher, 31 December 1952, LPL, Fisher Papers vol. 132, fo. 75.
[14] Hill to Fisher, 10 March 1953, LPL, Fisher Papers vol. 132, fo. 99.

shoulder to his right hip, intended perhaps as a visual aid to instruct his ordinands.

Archbishop Fisher believed that Wand's implacable attitude was clearly wrong, and complained to Archbishop Garbett of York that the Bishop of London 'would not budge'.[15] The two archbishops sought liberty of conscience, as Fisher explained: 'Both of us are satisfied that there is no legal requirement that a Stole must be worn at Ordination. Both of us are satisfied that however stupid it may be to refuse to wear a Stole it is a matter in which a man has a right to choose for himself whether to wear it or not.'[16] Likewise A. T. Houghton, in his appeal to Fisher on behalf of Elliott and Dunning, observed: 'if vestments of previous doubtful legality are to be authorised, every ordained minister of the Church ought to be allowed complete freedom to wear or not to wear them as his conscience dictates, and from the outset of his ministry.'[17]

This saga was eventually resolved at a meeting of bishops at Lambeth Palace in January 1953, when Wand agreed to relax his policy, to come in line with his brother bishops.[18]

---

[15] Fisher to Cyril Garbett, 1 December 1952, LPL, Fisher Papers vol. 109, fo. 87.

[16] Fisher to Wand, 5 November 1952, LPL, Fisher Papers vol. 109, fo. 65.

[17] A.T. Houghton to Fisher, 11 November 1952, LPL, Fisher Papers vol. 109, fo. 70

[18] Minutes of Bishops' Meetings, 12–13 January 1953, LPL, BM 13, fos 243–6.

'Every ordained minister of the Church ought to be allowed complete freedom to wear or not to wear them as his conscience dictates, and from the outset of his ministry.'

Fisher issued a formal statement of the episcopal consensus, as a guide to future Church of England policy:

> 1. Each Diocesan Bishop has sole responsibility for the men whom he accepts for Ordination, and is solely responsible for all the arrangements made for their Ordination, save for the fact that the Archdeacon who presents must also be satisfied that the persons presented are apt and meet for the ministry. Otherwise judgement as to a man's suitability and qualifications lies entirely within the Bishop's discretion.
>
> 2. As regards the wearing of a White Stole, for the future in no Diocese of the Church of England will an ordinand, who has been offered a title, be denied Ordination on the sole ground that he finds himself conscientiously unable to wear a white stole.
>
> 3. Where the question arises each Diocesan Bishop will ... meet the situation in his own way either by ordaining him himself without requiring a White Stole or by making some other provision for his Ordination.[19]

[19] 'The Use of the White Stole at Ordination', January 1953, LPL, Fisher Papers vol. 132, fo. 97.

This episcopal agreement, with its public affirmation of the inclusion of evangelical ordinands with tender consciences, was widely applauded. Donald Coggan thought that it admirably safeguarded 'both the freedom of conscience of the candidate, and the discipline of the Church'.[20] Stafford Wright was grateful for the bishops' gracious attitude and knew it would be 'a very great relief' to his ordinands at Tyndale Hall.[21] However, it still took a little while for all dioceses to embrace a permissive approach. David Pytches, a Tyndale Hall ordinand and later founder in the 1980s of the charismatic New Wine movement, was appointed as curate of St Ebbe's, Oxford in 1955. Since Pytches refused to wear a stole, the new Bishop of Oxford, Harry Carpenter, sent him to be ordained by Letters Dimissory in Rochester. The following year, the bishop finally relented and allowed him to take his place for presbyteral ordination at Christ Church cathedral in Oxford, stoleless.[22]

Clerical clothing remained a hotly contested question during the late 1950s and early 1960s, in the years leading up to the Clerical Vestments Measure of 1964 (now incorporated into Canon B8), which was the

---

[20] Donald Coggan to Fisher, 28 January 1953, LPL, Fisher Papers vol. 132, fo. 91.

[21] Stafford Wright to Fisher, 6 February 1953, LPL, Fisher Papers vol. 132, fo. 98.

[22] David Pytches, *Living at the Edge: Recollections and Reflections of a Lifetime* (Bath: Arcadia, 2002), 81.

firstfruits of Archbishop Fisher's revision of canon law.[23] It legalised albs, stoles and 'other customary vestments' for the first time since the Reformation, alongside the traditional surplice and black scarf, but also affirmed that the Church of England attached no 'particular doctrinal significance' to this diversity of vesture. It was widely welcomed as a permissive canon allowing greater liberty and choice in liturgical expression, with different traditions held together within the Church of England. The emphasis was upon freedom, rather than narrow conformity. During these wider debates, the question of stoles at ordination was again in the spotlight. As the draft Measure made its slow journey through the committees and councils of the Church Assembly, it was proposed to add a simple clause:

> No priest or deacon at his Ordination shall
> be required to wear a stole or vestments
> against his conscience.[24]

Those crafting the legislation declined to include this clause because the canon was focussed solely upon the vesture of clergy in their regular liturgical leadership and ordinands were outside that ambit. Nevertheless

---

[23] For the political implications of this Measure, see John Maiden and Peter Webster, 'Parliament, the Church of England and the Last Gasp of Political Protestantism, 1963–4', *Parliamentary History* 32 (June 2013): 361–77.

[24] Steering Committee Minutes, 13 November 1963, quoted in Michael Ramsey to Gerald Ellison, 21 January 1964, LPL, Ramsey Papers vol. 64, fo. 223.

they asked the House of Bishops to make it publicly known 'that nobody would be persecuted or penalised on account of his not wearing a stole at his Ordination'. Fisher's successor at Canterbury, Michael Ramsey, sought to reassure the church that 'none of the Bishops would require an ordinand to wear something contrary to his conscience'.[25]

The question of ordination stoles was broached in the Church Assembly, in the final debate over the Clerical Vestments Measure, where one speaker observed that 'in the past he knew that ordinands had been badgered and bullied and their consciences had been strained'.[26] But Bishop Ellison of Chester, at the urging of Archbishop Ramsey, gave public assurances that 'The Church of England was always meticulous in its defence of the conscience of its members. He was confident that no bishop would require an ordinand to wear a stole at his ordination if it were contrary to that man's conscience to do so.' He explained that the Vestments Measure was in any case meant to be permissive, legalising stoles and eucharistic vestments for the first time, not prescriptive by forcing these garments upon anybody. Therefore they need not worry that freedom for ordinands was not

---

[25] Ramsey to Ellison, 21 January 1964, LPL, Ramsey Papers vol. 64, fo. 224.
[26] Church Assembly, *Report of Proceedings*, vol. 44, 5 February 1964, 89 (Dr Morgan Williams).

made explicit in the legislation, since the issue would not arise.[27]

The same concerns were raised in both Houses of Parliament, before the legislation was sent forward for royal assent, and the same public assurances given. A number of MPs were concerned at the lack of explicit safeguards for ordinands, especially in the light of some past episcopal behaviour.[28] The case involving Elliott and Dunning was brought back to public attention in the pages of *The Daily Telegraph*.[29] In the House of Lords in July 1964, Viscount Brentford spoke of the 'very grave anxiety ... in the minds of a great many of us' that when stoles were legalised by the Measure, ordinands might be compelled to wear them at ordination 'contrary to their consciences'.[30] Archbishop Ramsey addressed Brentford's concerns head-on:

[27] Church Assembly, *Report of Proceedings*, vol. 44, 5 February 1964, 74.

[28] See 'Vestures of Ministers Measure', memorandum, 28 July 1964, LPL, Ramsey Papers vol. 64, fo. 225.

[29] Letter from John H. Potter (vicar of St John's, Upper Holloway), *Daily Telegraph*, 27 July 1964, 10, urging Parliament 'to safeguard liberty of conscience'. Potter, a friend of Elliott and Dunning at Oak Hill College, was one of those pressurised by Bishop Wand to wear a stole for his ordination at Michaelmas 1952.

[30] *Parliamentary Debates (Hansard): House of Lords*, 13 July 1964, vol. 260, column 33.

I can only say that from my knowledge of the Bench of Bishops, which is considerable, I think it is inconceivable that any of the Bishops would press an ordination candidate, contrary to his conscience, to wear a stole at his ordination. I believe it to be inconceivable. ... Because the purpose of this Measure is toleration, when it is passed I believe that Bishops and clergy and laity will be all the more anxious to put into practice the toleration which it enacts not only in the law but in the spirit as well; and that will be a tremendous gain for our Church.[31]

Freedom of conscience, permission not prescription, was likewise a keynote of the speech by the new Bishop of London (Robert Stopford) who was given responsibility for introducing the legislation in the Upper Chamber. He told the gathered peers:

I would emphasise again, my Lords, that the Measure is so worded that the alternatives are permissive and not compulsive, and that no clergyman could possibly be placed in a position where he would be forced to wear vestments to which he objected. ... It is comprehensive

---

[31] *Parliamentary Debates (Hansard): House of Lords*, 13 July 1964, vol. 260, columns 50–51.

> and it ensures that varieties of use are possible without departing from the doctrine of the Church of England. It ensures, too, that in mutual charity and toleration those varieties can be held together.[32]

In the House of Commons, the legislation was brought forward on behalf of the Church of England by Sir John Arbuthnot (the Second Church Estates Commissioner). He explained to his fellow MPs that this Measure was intended to allow greater freedom, in the spirit of Anglican comprehensiveness. None was under compulsion to use the new vestments:

> It is not a mandatory Measure, it is, rather, a permissive one, and in commending it to the House for approval I would just add that one of the great strengths of the Church of England is its tolerance. If given the choice of attending a service where the vestments were simple, or where they were more ornate, I would prefer the simple service every time, but I do not feel that it is up to me, who prefer simplicity, to deny more colourful

---

[32] *Parliamentary Debates (Hansard): House of Lords*, 13 July 1964, vol. 260, column 13.

> vestments to those who find them helpful
> in their worship.[33]

When it came to ordinands wearing stoles at ordination, Arbuthnot pointed to Ramsey's assurances already made in the House of Lords and to the bishops' 1953 guidelines. He declared that in the light of these episcopal and archiepiscopal promises about ordination stoles they should 'regard this question as closed'.[34] One MP wryly observed that since 'bishops and archbishops come and go' perhaps written legislation would be better than verbal assurances which are quickly forgotten by the next generation.[35]

The experience of subsequent decades demonstrates that we are indeed prone to forgetfulness. Of the forty-three diocesan bishops who oversaw the introduction of the Clerical Vestments Measure in 1964, just four of them were still sitting on the episcopal bench in 1978 when the principals of the evangelical theological colleges addressed Archbishop Coggan once again on 'the vexed question' of stoles at ordination. Previous assurances given to the Church Assembly and the Houses of Parliament, and laid down by the bishops' guidelines,

---

[33] *Parliamentary Debates (Hansard): House of Commons*, 30 July 1964, vol. 699, column 1869.

[34] *Parliamentary Debates (Hansard): House of Commons*, 30 July 1964, vol. 699, column 1870.

[35] *Parliamentary Debates (Hansard): House of Commons*, 30 July 1964, vol. 699, column 1883 (Captain Lawrence Orr, MP for South Down, Northern Ireland).

seemed to have been erased from the corporate episcopal memory. The evangelical principals observed that in the late 1970s, as in the early 1950s,

> several men have found themselves put under considerable pressure to conform and this sometimes during their ordination retreat. It is a sad thing if at such a time their thoughts have had to be taken up with matters of controversy, and it is especially distressing for a man who wants gladly to obey his bishop at the beginning of his ministry to be pressurised to do so at the expense of his own conscience.

The principals appealed to Coggan:

> It was understood that when the revised canons of our church legalised the different vestiary traditions within the Church of England there would be a greater acceptance of each other across the old divides, and many of us rejoice that this is so. ...

> It may be that some bishops who have been more recently appointed have not been aware of the freedom of conscience that has been allowed in the matter, and

in this case perhaps a reminder from you is all that is needed.[36]

Archbishop Coggan had a quiet word with the House of Bishops and the difficulty appeared to be settled, for the time being.[37]

And yet with every new generation of bishops, memories fade and so the difficulty returns. We need to remember our Anglican history. The guidelines agreed by the bishops in the 1950s, and publicly reaffirmed in the Church Assembly and the Houses of Parliament in the 1960s, are an excellent model of gracious episcopal policy. This pastoral breadth needs to be emulated today, so that in future no Anglican ordinands are put under pressure to wear a stole at ordination contrary to their consciences.

[36] John Cockerton (St John's College, Durham), J.P. Hickinbotham (Wycliffe Hall, Oxford), Keith Sutton (Ridley Hall, Cambridge), Alec Motyer (Trinity College, Bristol), Robin Nixon (St John's College, Nottingham) and David Wheaton (Oak Hill College) to Donald Coggan, 4 September 1978, LPL, Coggan Papers vol. 90, fos 166–7.
[37] Coggan to Cockerton, 12 February 1979, LPL, Coggan Papers vol. 90, fo. 169.

4. An Appeal

In light of the foregoing discussion, it is good for bishops in the Church of England to grant their ordinands freedom not to wear a stole at ordination. This appeal is based upon three key principles.

a) Conscience

For those evangelicals who reject the stole it is not a matter of partisanship, nor a desire to be awkward, nor in any way a sign of disloyalty to the bishop. Rather it is a matter of personal conscience, theologically informed, based upon their reading of Anglican history and the sacramental associations which are still attached to the stole. Bishops should not interpret evangelical reluctance to wear the stole as a challenge to their episcopal authority. On the contrary, it is only because ordinands feel conscience-bound that they are unable to follow the bishop's direction on this point. The ordination service is a solemn event in the life of any minister, after careful prayer and preparation, and includes the making of solemn vows before God and the church. How important it is, therefore, on this day of all days, that the consciences of ordinands are at ease.

b) Power

The relationship between bishop and ordinand is inevitably an uneven one, between the most senior member of the diocese and the most junior. The natural inclination of ordinands is therefore to seek the blessing and goodwill of the bishop in all things, and to want to build friendly collegiality. It is not easy for an ordinand to pluck up the courage to write to their bishop about stoles – perhaps to a bishop in a new diocese whom they have not yet met personally. No one wants a reputation as a troublemaker, least of all at the outset of their ministry. It is not a matter of canonical obedience, since canon law says nothing at all about vesture at ordinations.[1] Nonetheless, it is all too easy for bishops to use their authority to pressurise ordinands by signs of displeasure, exclusion, rebuke and insistence. This attitude can too easily become an abuse of power, browbeating junior clergy into acting against their consciences. Both the Church Assembly and the Houses of Parliament heard repeated assurances, by no less a dignitary than Archbishop Ramsey himself, that such episcopal pressure concerning vesture would never again be exerted upon Anglican ordinands.

c) Comprehension

The Church of England has enshrined in canon law an attitude of liberty and comprehension in matters of clerical dress. As has been seen, the intention of Canon B8 is to give permission for varieties of vesture – surplice and alb, scarf and stole – but not to enforce a particular

---

[1] See further, Gerald Bray, *The Oath of Canonical Obedience* (London: Latimer Trust, 2004); *To Proclaim Afresh: Declaration and Oaths for Church of England Ministers* (London: Church House Publishing, 2022).

Evangelical ordinands are asking to be included and welcomed within the diocese rather than made to feel like outsiders.

brand upon anybody. Evangelical ordinands are asking for that comprehension to be extended to them at ordination, to be included and welcomed within the diocese rather than made to feel like outsiders. As A. T. Houghton told Archbishop Fisher, it is a question of 'fairmindedness and fair play, to ensure liberty of conscience'.[2] Although stoles are worn in many churches today, this is not the universal Anglican practice, nor indeed the historic Anglican tradition, so it is wrong to enforce the stole upon everybody. For congregation members who come to the cathedral to support their new curate it is disconcerting to see them in a garment which is never worn in the local parish. After the painful crisis under Bishop Wand in the diocese of London, the bishops of the Church of England made it publicly known that henceforth every Anglican ordinand would be treated fairly and welcomed equally, whether or not they were willing to wear a stole. That episcopal consensus, reached corporately at Lambeth Palace after careful discussion, embodies the spirit of gracious comprehension in secondary matters of which Anglicans are rightly proud.

On these grounds, therefore, the bishops of the Church of England need to reconsider with care the practical instructions given to their curates at the time of ordination. The best practice, already modelled by several dioceses, is for all ordinands to be given the choice to wear a scarf or a stole, without having to ask

---

[2] Houghton to Fisher, 11 November 1952, LPL, Fisher Papers vol. 109, fo. 70.

for special permission. That freedom should be granted wholeheartedly, not grudgingly but with pleasure, and made explicit in the explanation of the ordination dress code. This permissive policy concerning scarf or stole enables the bishops and ordinands of the Church of England to work together in better harmony and mutual understanding, for the greater flourishing of the body of Christ and the extension of his kingdom.

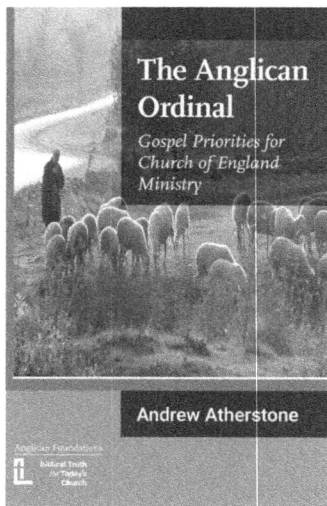

There is no better handbook for Anglican ministry than the Anglican ordinal – the authorised liturgy for ordaining new ministers. The ordinal contains a beautiful, succinct description of theological priorities and ministry models for today's church.

Andrew Atherstone's *The Anglican Ordinal* offers a simple exposition of the ordinal's primary themes. Anglican clergy are called to public ministry as messengers, sentinels, stewards, and shepherds. They are asked searching questions and they make solemn promises. The Holy Spirit's anointing is invoked upon their ministries, with the laying-on-of-hands, and they are gifted a Bible as the visual symbol of their new pastoral and preaching office. This booklet is a handy primer for ordinands and clergy, and all those responsible for their selection, training, and deployment.

Christian Leadership series

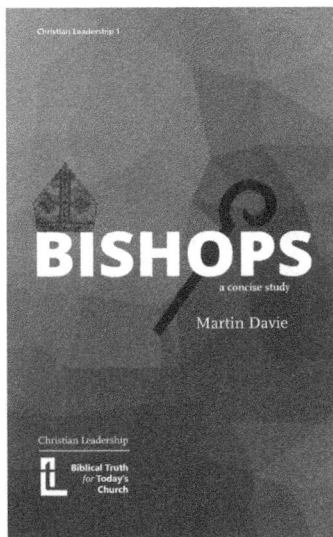

Bishops: A Concise Study summarises the key points of Martin Davie's major study *Bishops Past, Present and Future* (Gilead Books, 2022). It is designed to meet the needs of those who would like to know about the role and importance of bishops in the Church of England, but who would baulk at tackling the 800+ pages of the original book.

This concise study is published in the hope that it will help many in the Church of England, both ordained and lay, to think in a more informed fashion about how bishops should respond to the challenges and opportunities facing the Church of England at this critical point in its history.

Christian Leadership series

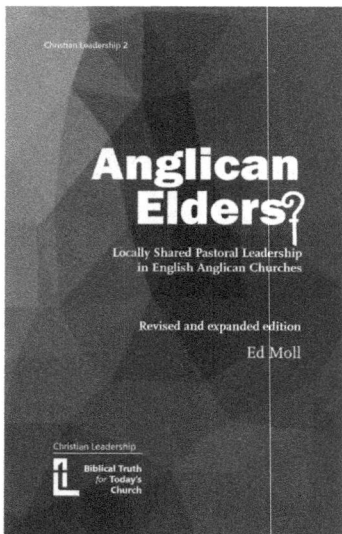

Anglican polity has traditionally favoured the incumbent as sole elder over a congregation. Biblical and missional imperatives press for eldership to be plural but how can this be done within an Anglican setting?

Ed Moll's *Anglican Elders?* explores the biblical and historical background to plural eldership or locally shared pastoral leadership. It goes on to describe the experience of nine UK Anglican pastors who have established a team that functions as a plural eldership. While the focus is on the church's ministry of making disciples, lessons are drawn for other areas of pastoral leadership.

The revised and expanded edition includes additional chapters on the role of women and on the place of power in pastoral ministry.